THE
TRESPASSERS

THE TRESPASSERS

MORRIS PANYCH

TALONBOOKS

Talonbooks
Box 2076, Vancouver, British Columbia, Canada V6B 3S3
www.talonbooks.com

Typeset in Meridien and printed and bound in Canada.
Printed on 100% post-consumer recycled paper.

First Printing: 2010

The publisher gratefully acknowledges the financial support of the Canada Council for the
Arts; the Government of Canada through the Book Publishing Industry Development
Program; and the Province of British Columbia through the British Columbia Arts Council
and the Book Publishing Tax Credit for our publishing activities.

Library and Archives Canada Cataloguing in Publication

Panych, Morris
  The trespassers / Morris Panych.

A play.
ISBN 978-0-88922-628-9

  I. Title.

PS8581.A65T74 2010   C812'.54   C2009-906979-2

The Trespassers premiered on July 26, 2009, at the Studio Theatre, as part of the Stratford Festival, Stratford, Ontario, with the following cast and crew:

CASH	Kelli Fox
MILTON	Robert King
ROXY	Lucy Peacock
LOWELL	Noah Reid
HARDY	Joseph Ziegler

Director	Morris Panych
Designer	Ken MacDonald
Lighting Designer	Jason Hand
Assistant Lighting Designer	Siobhán Sleath
Stage Manager	Ann Stuart
Assistant Stage Manager	Bruno Gonslaves
Production Assistant	Melissa Bergeron
Production Stage Manager	Marylu Moyer

1.

The play unfolds over the course of a few weeks, in some town in the middle of nowhere, not small enough to be a quaint place or large enough to be in any way an interesting one. They had a sawmill there, which was a going concern, but it has since shut down; it now crowns a sort of half-town, gutted of its reason for being. The story unfolds in many in town, moving in a generally chronological fashion; these events are recalled from the mind of LOWELL. Out of the darkness, an ungainly boy, fifteen years of age, appears in the middle of a police interview, holding a peach. Nearby, RCMP OFFICER MILTON takes notes.

LOWELL: Between just the two of us, we could collect a dozen peaches in one haul. A dozen is twelve, which is a religious number, based on the Apostles.

MILTON: Okay, a dozen.

LOWELL: A baker's dozen is thirteen. *Thou shalt not steal* is the Sixth Commandment. I believe it's the Sixth Commandment. Or it's the Seventh. My mother made me memorize them.

CASH, a tired woman in her late thirties, appears.

CASH: I didn't.

LOWELL: And you have to listen to your mother. That's the Fourth Commandment.

MILTON: Lying, what about that?

LOWELL: Technically, not a sin.

MILTON: Bearing false witness against your neighbour, or something like that?

CASH: Neighbour means *anybody*.

HARDY: There's something in-between lying and not lying. It's called a story.

MILTON: What about murder? Isn't that a Commandment?

LOWELL considers.

CASH: It's a Commandment.

LOWELL: Murder is the Fifth. And it isn't just a person. It can count if it's a frog, say—if you killed it for no reason. That's what I believe.

CASH: You won't get a straight answer.

LOWELL: Or—or—hunting, unless you eat it after; or you could freeze it. But stealing, that's—besides, even if it was on somebody else's property, it isn't stealing if the peach falls from the tree; that's what my grandfather said.

MILTON: What your grandfather said, okay.

HARDY appears, a wiry old man in a straw hat, carrying a stack of newspapers.

HARDY: Anything that isn't attached to something else belongs to God.

LOWELL: You don't believe in God.

HARDY: Don't I?

LOWELL: You're an atheist, Grandpa.

HARDY: You'll find, as you get older, God starts to slip into the conversation.

LOWELL: I'd like to be old.

HARDY: Just don't ever get the feeling that you've lived too long.

LOWELL: I won't.

HARDY: I'm going to the shed for a bit. Say nothing to your mother on the subject.

LOWELL: My grandfather had a stash of newspaper clippings out there, which he took out of their folders and read. My mother called it unseemly.

CASH: Trash.

LOWELL: He listened to his old records out there. He collected stories about crime. Murder, mostly, but also grand larceny, rape, a story about a man who cut off his balls by accident, only it didn't say balls, it said "a disfiguring accident involving an olive press."

Strains of an old recording.

HARDY: You need to read between the lines.

9

LOWELL: Sometimes he'd let me look at his clippings. On a hot day, say. When it was too hot for peach expeditions, or going down to the trough. Horses used to water there, in the old days. You could just imagine. You could.

HARDY: A guy gets off his horse, dips his hat in, pours cool water over his head.

LOWELL: Were you ever a cowboy?

HARDY: I knew one. Buster Hinkey. Rode in the rodeo. But he fell off a mountain—blown clean off in a sudden gust of wind. That's the way to go: a sudden gust of wind, Lowell. Don't stick around for the details.

LOWELL: Mom says she can hardly wait for you to drop dead.

The music stops.

MILTON: Your mother said that.

CASH: I never said that.

HARDY: Your mother has a way with words.

LOWELL: Ever since Dad left, Mom had it in for my grandfather.

CASH wears a security guard uniform from the local Museum of Forestry.

CASH: And that is also not true.

LOWELL: It's all very psychological.

CASH: Is that a peach?

LOWELL: I'm not sure.

CASH: Did your grandfather put you up to this?

LOWELL: He says they're fair play.

CASH: Not from someone else's property.

LOWELL: They don't even live here anymore.

CASH: Doesn't matter.

LOWELL: It's the redistribution of wealth.

CASH: There's no such thing.

LOWELL: They're just lying there on the ground, Mom. Do you call that an equitable situation?

CASH: A what?

LOWELL: If somebody doesn't use something, then they shouldn't have it, and that's final.

CASH: I don't have the energy for you, Lowell. Go find something useful to do.

LOWELL: Everything I do around here is practically illegal.

CASH: If it involves a rifle again, yes.

MILTON: Tell me about the rifle.

LOWELL: I took it out so Grandpa could teach me how to aim.

HARDY appears with a rifle.

11

HARDY: Cock your head slightly to the side; that's it. Pay attention; this is a dangerous weapon.

LOWELL: You said "cock."

HARDY: You should be able to see clearly the two sights of the rifle. That's how you line it up.

MILTON: What did you shoot?

HARDY: Steady hand, steady hand. See if you can hit the letter *o*.

LOWELL: We tried to shoot the *r* completely out of the sign and make the *v* into an *r* so it would say "pirate property."

MILTON: So you're a pretty good shot then.

LOWELL: No.

A gunshot, distant, but distinct.

HARDY: Looks more like "primate property" now.

LOWELL: Sometimes we shot at peaches, to watch them explode.

HARDY shoots.

HARDY: Beautiful.

LOWELL: Besides, what else is there to do in this thankless valley?

MILTON: You tell me.

LOWELL: You tell me.

MILTON: Oh. I'm sorry. Are you asking the questions, now?

LOWELL: Why do we live here anyway, Grandpa?

HARDY: Somebody had to.

LOWELL: Sitting on a porch all day is about it. Grandpa calls this booger country.

HARDY: Nose picking—it's about the only industry left.

CASH: Don't you have any friends?

LOWELL: No.

CASH: What have you done all day?

LOWELL: You know.

CASH: What about that boy who just moved in? That one with the what do you call it—

LOWELL: Weird head? (*out*) A boy moved to our town. It was a singular experience. No one has moved here since anyone can remember; they only just move out. But he moved in with his family and his weird head. They started a grocery but nobody goes there—ever.

CASH: Don't say "weird head."

LOWELL: (*to CASH*) His ears are too low; have you noticed? Grandpa says it's from being amphibian. Did you know that we are descended from sea creatures? We're at the forward end of an evolutionary process, but if something goes haywire in the womb, it's what happens—a reversion to am-phib-ianism. That's why you look exactly like a fish before you're born—because you're

13

not even a human being yet, just evolving into one, basically.

CASH: A fetus is a human being.

LOWELL: That's not what Grandpa says.

CASH: Your grandfather is going to Hell.

LOWELL: Hell is completely full.

HARDY: Not even the Pope could get in now.

CASH: Whatever happened to that girl from the apartments? She's nice.

LOWELL: Her father got arrested.

CASH: He did?

LOWELL: Anyway, their house smells like pee.

CASH: No it doesn't.

LOWELL: How would you know?

CASH: I just know.

LOWELL: It smells like pee. I'm telling you. All the boys in one room and they all pee the bed; there's five of them in there. Five boys in one room. You should see it. It's a dereliction of social mores.

CASH: Is that right?

LOWELL: By the way, is it okay to jack off with another person?

CASH: Oh my God.

LOWELL: Just asking.

CASH: What are you talking about? No it is not okay! It's not okay.

LOWELL: I thought that would be your reaction. I meant to ask Grandpa, but he won't discuss sex with me. He says it's better if I find out on my own through trial and error.

CASH: I can't talk about this.

LOWELL: That's alright. I appreciate your candour.

CASH: Candour is not the right word to use, Lowell. Stop eating that peach. Are you doing something that you shouldn't be doing?

LOWELL: No.

CASH: Then why did you ask about that—business?

LOWELL: I was invited to join a club is all.

CASH: What sort of club?

LOWELL: Just a club.

CASH: Look at me. Come here. Look at me. What do they do in this club?

LOWELL: Mostly they take their clothes off and stuff, but they also play thirty-one and smoke menthols.

CASH: They do not! Who's in this club?

LOWELL: There's some guys. And some girls.

CASH: Girls, too?

LOWELL: I don't know all the exact inside details, Mom. I'm not even an initiate. They told me first I have to pass a series of humiliating personal tests of my character.

CASH: Are kids making you do things you shouldn't again?

LOWELL: It's just an innocent blossoming.

CASH: You are not playing cards with a bunch of naked boys and girls. Believe me, there are far more innocent ways of blossoming in this world.

LOWELL: I'm at the sexually curious stage; it's an awkward and difficult time.

CASH: You're not at any such stage, young man, any such stage. Sex is for marriage.

LOWELL: Okay.

CASH: Besides, those kids just want to make fun of you.

LOWELL: No they don't.

HARDY: No they don't.

CASH: And if you are at that—stage, then—then I think you should talk to someone who can help. The minister. I have to get to work.

LOWELL: It's Sunday.

CASH: Is it?

LOWELL: Are you sneaking off to church again?

CASH is gone.

LOWELL: Mom was trying to pretend she wasn't a Christian.

MILTON: Why pretending?

HARDY appears, with magazines.

HARDY: Opiate for the masses.

LOWELL: Grandpa didn't want any Christians in our house.

HARDY: Never talk to a minister about sex, Lowell, unless you don't want to have any. I suppose I'll have to step in here. Have you ever been to a prostitute?

LOWELL: I'm only fifteen.

HARDY: Well, I'll have to show you some pictures then.

LOWELL: Grandpa showed me pictures, from his private collection.

HARDY: People who don't like this call it pornography.

LOWELL: I've seen pictures like this before, Grandpa; believe me.

HARDY: Of course you have, but not in any objective way. Let me just start by saying, these are not naked women, Lowell. These are pictures of naked women. There's a difference. In order for a woman to have her picture taken, she had to strip in front of a camera. I want you to think about that.

LOWELL: Okay.

HARDY: It's a non-union job.

LOWELL: Is it?

HARDY: You can rely on these for pleasure but not for any lasting satisfaction. I recommend this one here. It'll give you a few unexpected biological insights. That's a labia.

LOWELL: Gee.

HARDY: Try to remember, while viewing this, that this, here, is also the passage through which children are brought into the world; you yourself entered through such a passage. It's a miraculous place, Lowell. Covet it and respect it, simultaneously.

CASH: (*re-entering*) Are you completely out of your—are you out of your ever-loving mind?

HARDY: I can't stop the free flow of information.

CASH: It's getting to the point where I can't trust you alone with him. Where's my I.D. badge?

HARDY: You can trust me.

CASH: You think it's clever to treat him like an adult.

HARDY: The boy is gifted in ways you don't know.

CASH: See? You put that kind of idea in his head; it makes him think he's invincible. It's dangerous. You know how reckless he can get.

HARDY: He's been misdiagnosed. That is, if you want my medical opinion.

CASH: I don't.

HARDY: Quit trying to control him. You turn him into a dullard, a vacant parking lot.

CASH: I'm trying to help him.

HARDY: Mind control, that's all that is. You can't control people, Cash. That's part of your problem. You want to control people.

CASH: No I don't. I do not. Control people?

HARDY: What about Connor?

CASH: What about him?

HARDY: I only mention him.

CASH: In a conversation about me wanting to control people.

HARDY: Draw your own conclusions.

CASH: Connor was sleeping with another woman.

HARDY: So what?

CASH: So what?

HARDY: He was redefining himself in the context of his redundancy.

CASH: What?

HARDY: It's what men do. In the context of their redundancy, they redefine themselves.

CASH: Not all men.

HARDY: Blame capitalism.

CASH: Worse than that, he lied and he kept on lying. I can live with a cheater, but I can't live with a liar.

HARDY: The problem with marriage, you see—the problem with marriage—

CASH: Actually, what am I saying? I can't live with a liar *or* a cheater.

HARDY: You can't live with the simple truth is what you can't live with. Men are men. And women are not.

CASH: Gosh, that is simple.

HARDY: I slept with other women.

CASH: You did not.

HARDY: How do you know?

CASH: You're my father and you did not sleep with other women. And if you did sleep with other women, you can leave this house and never speak to me again. You never slept with other women.

HARDY: It's my house by the way. Small point.

CASH: Fine, then I'll leave.

HARDY: You know that's not going to happen.

CASH: No?

HARDY: You've got a good thing going here.

CASH: Oh, right. I forgot. I've got a good thing going here. I live in a mill town with no mill, work in a museum that nobody visits, and my husband left me for a woman half my height.

HARDY: Half your age is what I think you mean to say.

CASH: While Mom was still alive?

HARDY: Eh?

CASH: I do *not* try to control people.

HARDY: Lithium. That's mind control. Every child is a normal child; it's the parents that fuck 'em up.

CASH: That word.

HARDY: I'm trying to expand the boy's horizons. The kid doesn't even know how to play with himself.

CASH: If you can't look after him, properly, I'll just have to make other plans.

HARDY: What other plans?

CASH: Other plans.

HARDY: I'll look after him. Don't you worry.

CASH: What are you doing with those magazines anyway? I don't want to know. Aren't you a bit old? Is that a peach?

HARDY: This?

CASH: I'm warning you, Dad. The police have been here twice already.

HARDY: Have they nothing better to do?

CASH: You've been warned. It's private property.

HARDY: That is an abandoned orchard.

CASH: That belongs to someone else.

HARDY: Peaches, rotting. Is that what we have police for? To protect abandoned fruit? Corporate thugs, that's what they are.

MILTON: Your grandfather was a troublemaker, wasn't he? A real shit-disturber?

LOWELL: My grandfather had principles and I guess some other people just don't.

CASH: Dad, I'm not going to have this argument again. Stay away from those peaches, or you'll find yourself in jail.

HARDY: Good.

CASH: I don't have the money to bail you out.

HARDY: Good.

CASH: Fine.

LOWELL: Mom made my grandfather swear on his own grave not to go over that fence again.

CASH: And that goes for you too.

LOWELL: I didn't even know I had a grave.

LOWELL deals out some cards; we are in the downtown rooms of ROXY, HARDY's sometime-girlfriend.

HARDY: Not a grave, specifically, but you've got a death awaiting you. The date is already set. When you pick them up, don't look at them right away. You want to seem confident and, at the same time, see if your opponent reacts to his hand in any telling way; if his pupils dilate, he's got at least a pair of queens. The next move is yours. The thing about cards is you get what you're dealt, but how you deal with them defines your character.

ROXY, a hard woman about forty-five years old, appears with drinks.

ROXY: Tequila can be a hallucinogen, if used correctly.

HARDY: We all know that. (*to LOWELL*) I'd fold if I were you.

LOWELL: Why?

HARDY: You can't beat me.

LOWELL: What makes you so sure?

ROXY: I don't go in for this salt/lime thing. Just a waste of my time.

HARDY: What are you doing?

LOWELL: Folding?

HARDY: Why?

LOWELL: You said I should.

ROXY: Never believe an old man, sweetie.

HARDY: Don't play what's in your hand.

ROXY: Let him do what he wants.

HARDY: If I teach him nothing else before I die, I'm going to teach him how to bluff. Bluffing is humankind at his finest. It involves two completely contradictory aspects of thought: knowing and not knowing. Between the two, Lowell, lies the sublime.

ROXY: He'll say anything to win a hand of poker.

HARDY: Did anybody ask you?

LOWELL: What if my cards aren't very good?

HARDY: Don't tell me that. He tells me his hand isn't very good. Don't tell me that.

LOWELL: Okay.

HARDY: Like I said, Lowell, it's got absolutely nothing to do with what's in your hand. It's what's in your mind that counts. That you can control. What's in your hand is what's in your hand. Make me think you're holding three aces.

LOWELL: How?

HARDY: When you look at your cards, let your head go back just slightly and widen your eyes a little; keep scanning the cards, as if you can't quite believe your good luck. Bet tentatively at first, then lean back. Try to act unexcited. That's good. I see you and raise you.

LOWELL: Can you beat three aces?

HARDY: No, but I know you're trying to bluff me, now.

LOWELL: Then I fold.

HARDY: Don't fold. Make me doubt my own wisdom. Great men make little men doubt. That's how Lenin came to power, and Stalin after him. Bet, and bet high. Churchill, now there was a bluffer.

LOWELL: I'll lose all my money.

HARDY: Losing or winning isn't the point.

ROXY: No?

HARDY: You want to be a victim of your own fate?

LOWELL: No.

ROXY: He doesn't know what that means. Do you know what that means, sweetie?

HARDY: He knows what it means.

ROXY: Another shot of tequila and he'll definitely know.

HARDY: Two is the limit at his age.

LOWELL: I bet it all; I'm all in.

HARDY: Don't be a fool; you know you can't beat me.

LOWELL: But I want it to be over.

HARDY: I give up. How am I ever supposed to teach you how to play cards? I call. What've you got?

LOWELL lays down his hand.

LOWELL: Three kings and two nines.

ROXY: Full house.

   Beat.

HARDY: You were going to fold.

LOWELL: I was bluffing.

ROXY: That's a full house.

HARDY: We all know that's a full house, Roxy. You needn't
   go on about it. Young man, that was a completely
   underhanded move. I applaud you for it.

LOWELL: Grandpa taught me how to bluff, which came in
   quite handy at times.

MILTON: Like now?

CASH: Is that booze on your breath?

LOWELL: Bluffing isn't lying. Bluffing is failing to supply the
   correct information, while purposely misleading the
   opponent. Lying is different. Lying is saying something
   that isn't true at the moment, but could be at some point.
   I forgot to say; Freddy's mother died.

MILTON: So is this bluffing or lying?

LOWELL: This is the story, sir …

CASH: She did?

LOWELL: Cancer.

CASH: Who's Freddy?

LOWELL: That—friend of mine.

CASH: Which friend?

LOWELL: You know. The Jehovah's Witness.

CASH: I never heard of a Freddy.

LOWELL: He's that really nice kid, you know, who likes to read all the time.

CASH: You have a friend who likes to read?

LOWELL: It was Grandpa's idea that I not just invent a friend, but a friend with an acceptable profile.

HARDY: That way you won't worry the poor woman unnecessarily if you have to go out and do something you're not supposed to.

CASH: Are you sure he wants you to stay over? His mother just died.

LOWELL: We're going to sleep in a tent and tell ghost stories.

CASH: Isn't that a little morbid?

LOWELL: He could use the company.

CASH: Let's not have a repeat of last year.

LOWELL: Last year I slept over at Barry Benjamin's house and we snuck out and took all the washing off everybody's line and threw it in their gardens and jumped on it; it was Barry's idea. (*to CASH*) Barry was Jewish, Mom. Freddy is a Presbyterian.

CASH: I thought you said he was a Jehovah's Witness.

LOWELL: Yeah. Remembering your story is a lot harder than making it up in the first place. I had to say they were Jehovah's Witness in case she wondered why they never went to our church. (*to CASH*) He's thinking of converting.

CASH: That's nice.

HARDY: Good construction. It's the only difference between a lie and a short story.

LOWELL: I told Mom that Freddy was a diabetic, so that I had to take him chocolate bars all the time. I told her that his sister was a dog trainer because I saw one on T.V.

HARDY: Base your stories on real life.

LOWELL: And that his Dad, of course, was an immigrant from Mexico, which would explain the tequila smell.

CASH: I thought Jehovah's Witnesses didn't drink.

LOWELL: Give the guy a break, Mom.

CASH: Poor man. Maybe he'd like to come over for dinner sometime.

LOWELL: He's not looking for a new wife, just yet.

CASH: I was only trying to be nice.

LOWELL: Maybe once he's through the worst, he'll have the strength to love again.

CASH: I'm not looking for a husband, thank you, Lowell. Mexican, Jehovah's Witness, or otherwise.

LOWELL: Why not?

CASH: One was enough.

HARDY: She's overcompensating for her fears of rejection. We have to convince her not to let herself go. It's important for a woman to remain beautiful in spite of everything.

CASH: I'm not letting myself go. Do you think I'm letting myself go?

LOWELL: You used to wear make-up more.

CASH: I should get my hair done.

LOWELL: Ever since Dad—she stopped getting her hair done. That was over a year ago. Now all she says is, "I should get my hair done," but she never does. Should I tell you the story about Dad?

MILTON: We'll get to that.

LOWELL: Okay.

MILTON: Tell me more about the girlfriend.

LOWELL: Roxy.

ROXY appears in the foreground, in her robe.

ROXY: Your grandfather thought I should talk to you.

LOWELL: Okay.

ROXY: You know how to give yourself pleasure, right? Don't worry; for men, it's a good thing.

LOWELL: What about for women?

ROXY: For women, it's just a lot of work—especially at my age. Frankly, I get more pleasure reading a magazine. But for men, it gives them a brief period of reflection in an otherwise tight schedule of aggression.

LOWELL: Is it a sin?

ROXY: No, but in some venues it's against the law.

LOWELL: Wow.

ROXY: Personally, I don't think anything should be against the law.

LOWELL: Not even murder?

ROXY: Nope.

LOWELL: What about the Ten Commandments?

ROXY: Well, I don't know about those; but crimes only exist because there are laws. If there were no laws there would be no crimes. You see what I'm saying?

LOWELL: What's to stop people from doing wrong?

ROXY: People know; in their hearts they know not to do wrong.

LOWELL: What about criminals?

ROXY: There are no criminals, just people who commit crimes.

LOWELL: So why do they commit crimes?

ROXY: Because in their hearts they feel they should be in jail.

LOWELL: You ever been to jail?

ROXY: It's just part of living.

CASH: (*furious*) I don't believe it!

HARDY: It was innocence personified.

CASH: She was giving him a lecture on masturbation!

HARDY: Somebody has to; why not call in the experts.

CASH: Experts?

HARDY: She's done some counselling.

CASH: Where?

HARDY: She has a radio show.

CASH: You are not to be entrusted with that boy—ever again.

HARDY: Fine. I'll take him fishing.

CASH: No. No, you won't. Because that is the end of this unholy alliance. Lowell is too young and too impressionable and too vulnerable to be exposed to this sort of thing. Who is this woman?

HARDY: I've told you about her. Roxy.

CASH: You've never told me anything about any Roxy. What is she? A girlfriend?

HARDY: Paramour.

CASH: Honestly.

HARDY: She's very much her own woman.

CASH: Lowell is going to a camp. I've decided. And in the fall, I'm sending him—

Beat.

HARDY: Where?

CASH: There's a school.

HARDY: Where?

CASH: Never mind where; there's a school.

HARDY: A school.

CASH: It's for people with special educational needs.

HARDY: He has no special educational needs. He has ordinary educational needs, just like everybody else. If you treat him like he's fucked-up in the head, he'll act like it.

CASH: Don't use that—please, Dad. Lowell has a mental problem that neither you nor I is at all equipped to deal with. I have a full-time job and the only person who can look after him is you. If he was a normal boy, it might not matter so much. But he's liable to do more damage to himself if he stays here. He's already tried to commit suicide.

HARDY: That wasn't exactly suicide.

CASH: What was it, then?

HARDY: We were supposed to come in right away and find him; he told me. It was a practical joke.

CASH: Is that what he told you?

HARDY: The joke went a little wrong.

CASH: What's more, I can't trust you with his medication.

HARDY: Why not?

CASH: For one thing, you've been convincing him not to take it; now look at him.

HARDY: What's wrong with him?

LOWELL appears, remarkably changed in mood.

LOWELL: Nothing!

HARDY: There's nothing wrong with him.

LOWELL: Quit saying there's something wrong with me. Maybe there's something wrong with you!

MILTON: That might be the case; but we're talking about you at the moment.

LOWELL: Quit talking about me then.

MILTON: Alright.

LOWELL: I want to go home now.

MILTON: That's not possible for the time being.

LOWELL cries; MILTON disappears. His mother appears to comfort him.

CASH: There's my baby. There's my baby.

HARDY: He's not a baby.

LOWELL: I'm not a baby.

CASH: I know you aren't. But you were once, and sometimes that's just how I see you. It's a mother's prerogative.

LOWELL: I'm not going to a summer camp.

CASH: It's on a lake.

LOWELL: They're all Christians; I'm an atheist.

CASH: No you're not. Grandpa's just put that idea into your head. Young boys can't be atheists.

LOWELL: Why not?

CASH: They just can't be. It would make the world too sad.

LOWELL: The world is sad.

CASH: Take your medication and it won't be.

ROXY appears with a bucket of quarters.

ROXY: Mothers are seldom wrong about their children. If you were my son, I'd shove that medication down your throat.

HARDY: No you wouldn't.

ROXY: I'd shove it down yours as well.

HARDY: What's this?

ROXY: Coins for the slots. What does it look like?

HARDY: They don't call those one-arm bandits for nothing, Lowell.

LOWELL: There's a casino on the reservation.

CASH: Casino?

LOWELL: We took a bus.

HARDY: No opponent, where's the fun in that? Gambling against a machine. You want an opponent.

ROXY: I wouldn't take betting advice from your grandfather.

HARDY: Stay away from numbers; there's just too many of them. You want a game where you can face your enemy down. Blackjack.

ROXY: House has the advantage.

HARDY: House always has the advantage.

LOWELL: Grandpa was the union representative; did I say that? Industrial Wood and Allied Workers. He negotiated for the union because he was so good at bluffing.

HARDY: I stood those boys down.

LOWELL: That's why things ended up the way they ended up in our town.

CASH: No it's not.

LOWELL: He bluffed so well, the company folded.

HARDY: They think I let them down.

CASH: The mill closed for other reasons.

LOWELL: To this day, a lot of those guys won't speak to him at all. Like if they saw him in the bar, they would move tables just not to be near him—the ones that still lived here, that is.

HARDY appears with two beers.

HARDY: Look at this place—empty as a tomb.

LOWELL: Should I be drinking this?

HARDY: It's beer, for Christ's sake.

LOWELL: You were just trying to make their lives better. Right?

HARDY: Workers are commodities. One day they outlive their usefulness. Until that day, they have one card and one card only to play. Unity, you can't beat that. Once one mill capitulates, then another capitulates. Then they all capitulate. We stood our ground here. The other mills may still be open, sure, but here we stood our ground.

LOWELL: It's kind of sour.

HARDY: It's a sourness you'll learn to appreciate. Don't watch her like she's a sideshow. You got to pay attention by not paying attention. She's a stripper, not a conundrum.

MILTON: They didn't throw you out of there?

LOWELL: It was dark.

HARDY: Besides, they need the business. You're drinking that too fast.

LOWELL: I can't say I like it.

HARDY: Wait for the buzz.

LOWELL: Okay.

He stumbles. CASH appears.

CASH: Are you alright?

HARDY: He'll be fine. Too much sun.

CASH: It's raining.

HARDY: Too much rain.

CASH: He's been drinking.

HARDY: A couple of beers is not drinking.

CASH: He leaves Monday. That's it.

LOWELL pukes.

Camp.

HARDY: Listen to me, Lowell; your mother is determined to brainwash you. We have little time left.

LOWELL: Where are we going?

HARDY: Where I've always dreamed of going, that's where.

LOWELL: Grandpa had never been out of our town his whole life, so where he dreamed of going was just about anywhere. At first it was a little confusing. We were going to steal an airplane, but then that didn't seem practical since we couldn't fly it; so we opted for stealing a car. Mom's car. We drove only a little ways out of town, then Grandpa pulled over and just stopped the car. He didn't say anything; just turned off the ignition and sat there.

Beat.

LOWELL: Grandpa?

HARDY: That's about it, I guess.

LOWELL: That's all he said. I don't think he was even talking to me.

HARDY: Eh?

LOWELL: I didn't say anything.

HARDY: The world's too big for us.

LOWELL: Then we drove back again.

HARDY: Let's cut through the orchard.

LOWELL: The Andersons are rich people who used to live here a long time ago, but they moved away even before the mill closed. They left their big house and the peach orchard and everything; didn't even look back. Officially, nobody is allowed into their estate. Some of the older kids have snuck in and out of there, but trespassing is strictly prohibited, which Grandpa says is suspect. He says that if there's a sign, then they are aware of our existence, and therefore liable; he's studied the law.

HARDY: Nor do we have any clear case of *trespass de bonis asportatis*, because the owner would have to prove that the peaches brought him any enjoyment.

LOWELL: The Andersons have other property in other towns. But they don't visit those, either.

HARDY: The natives never owned anything, except their own souls. White men came and introduced the concept of property. It's a convenient way of stealing. Look at those peaches up there. Get me that ladder.

LOWELL: I thought we only took peaches from the ground.

HARDY: This is anticipatory reclamation; they'll fall sooner or later, so it's legitimate in this case to take them now— prevents bruising. It's like all the best things in life, Lowell.

LOWELL: It is?

HARDY: You take a thing before it falls to ruin. We're rescuing these peaches from the dull tragedy of their long decay. This ladder is unsafe; duly noted. Criminal negligence.

LOWELL: I should go up.

MILTON: Why didn't you?

HARDY: I need you catching. An accurate eye, below. Besides, if somebody comes along, you can high-tail it out of here; I can't.

LOWELL: What'll you do?

HARDY: I'll hide in the tree until they're gone. I have excellent camouflage skills—on account of my empathy for my natural surroundings. The older you get, the more you become like the things around you—fade into the ethos.

CASH: If only that were true.

ROXY: Don't ask me. I'm just going with the flow.

CASH serves ROXY a cup of tea.

CASH: It's not that I mind him—you know—being curious. Boys are naturally curious.

ROXY: Girls aren't?

CASH: I think you know what I mean.

ROXY: Is this—tea?

CASH: Uh—

ROXY: Little late in the day.

CASH: I'm sorry. I don't have anything else.

ROXY: I do.

ROXY produces a mickey of whiskey; she pours some in CASH's tea.

CASH: I don't drink.

ROXY: You do now. Live a little.

CASH: Thank you.

ROXY: And no, I don't know what you mean. I was always curious. Weren't you?

CASH: Not about that.

ROXY: About what?

CASH: That.

ROXY: Sex? You weren't curious about sex?

CASH: Lowell has a borderline emotional disorder.

ROXY: Yeah, I heard about that.

CASH: He's been diagnosed. He's bipolar.

ROXY: Hardy says it's a misdiagnosis.

CASH: My father is not a doctor. Lowell has been examined and determined to have a mood disorder. He was prescribed a drug, which helps to keep his moods even.

ROXY: That's one way to raise a kid.

CASH: Why should he suffer unnecessarily?

ROXY: Is that why you asked me here? To talk about Lowell's moods?

CASH: I was curious about you. Dad never told me he had a—paramour.

ROXY: A what?

CASH: How long have you known him?

ROXY: Long enough.

CASH: Before my mother died?

ROXY: Your mother was a wonderful woman.

CASH: You knew her?

ROXY: Never met her. Just trying to change the subject.

CASH: I can't believe my father would have an extramarital affair.

ROXY: (*off of CASH's look*) Your mother was ill for a long time.

CASH: All the same—

ROXY: His heart was broken. I offered myself for comfort. He accepted. This rye isn't half bad with a bit of tea in it.

CASH: I want you to help me with Lowell.

ROXY: How?

HARDY: Catch!

CASH: I want him to let go of his grandfather.

ROXY: Really?

LOWELL: Careful, Grandpa.

HARDY: Catch!

ROXY: Why?

LOWELL: I needed to extricate myself from his questionable influence.

MILTON: So you killed him.

LOWELL: Yes.

ROXY: It's a pretty solid friendship.

MILTON: Can you repeat that answer for me, Lowell.

LOWELL: I said, "Yes."

MILTON: Yes.

CASH: I'm only trying to keep him—safe. He's learning all the wrong things. He only listens to his grandfather. He contradicts teachers at school. He gets into fights.

LOWELL: She said Wellington defeated Napoleon, Mom.

CASH: Well, didn't he?

LOWELL: Wellington's soldiers defeated Napoleon's soldiers.

CASH: Isn't that the same thing?

HARDY: Those teachers are training monkeys.

LOWELL: An army is made up of soldiers.

HARDY: The generals are always at the rear.

LOWELL: I'm a soldier.

HARDY: That's right.

CASH: How are you a soldier?

HARDY: You're in the front line of the battle, kid.

LOWELL: Against capitalism.

CASH: You don't even know what capitalism is.

HARDY: It's what destroyed this town.

CASH: It's what built this town.

HARDY: She has a point.

LOWELL: You have a point, Mom.

HARDY: But just because you make a thing doesn't give you a right to destroy it. The inhabitors are the rightful owners of property. They stopped the mill workers from starting up their own corporation here. It could have worked. It could have saved this town. It could have saved this town.

ROXY: He still going on about that?

LOWELL: Yeah.

ROXY: Lately, he seems to only talk about things that happened instead of things that are happening. Not that there's any difference in this town. All the same, I'd do anything for that man. He rescued me from a life of utter ruin. His words, but anyways it's true. He's the one who got me a job at the radio. And closer to my chosen field.

LOWELL: You don't say.

ROXY: I'm working my way towards a singing career. Only need the one thing.

LOWELL: A voice. That's what Grandpa says.

ROXY: I need a band, Lowell. A band is all I need—just a little three-piece combo. I write all my own tunes. All they need to do is play them.

LOWELL: He showed me a picture of you, naked, except for a baseball hat.

ROXY: I don't know why he has that picture. I look like somebody's mother.

LOWELL: Not mine.

ROXY: I suppose he thinks you could use a little hands-on education.

LOWELL shrugs.

Poor kid.

LOWELL: I'm not a kid.

ROXY: I promised your mother I would be a better influence.

LOWELL: Yeah?

She opens her robe and without ceremony draws his hand up to her naked breast.

LOWELL: It's soft, sort of.

ROXY: Well, that's good news. Any other insights?

LOWELL: How much do you think it weighs?

ROXY: Never weighed it. Don't worry. It won't be on the exam.

LOWELL: I don't know what else to say.

ROXY: Don't have to say anything. They're just tits.

She closes the robe.

ROXY: Why are men so interested in tits, I have to ask
myself.

LOWELL: Don't know.

ROXY: Of course you don't. It's one of those eternal
questions. But hey, thank goodness; otherwise they'd pay
no attention to us whatsoever. They're like stone; men
are the immovable object that women move. I heard that
someplace, or else I made it up. In any case, it's going in
my book.

LOWELL: You're writing a book.

ROXY: No. I know way too much.

She begins opening her robe again.

So, ever seen one of these before?

CASH: That's it. That is the last straw.

HARDY: You're in danger of losing your sense of humour.

CASH: Sense of humour? She exposed her naked body!

HARDY: She doesn't mind; she's an artist's model.

CASH: I thought she worked in radio.

HARDY: She does a lot of things.

CASH: He's not old enough to be looking at naked women and touching their breasts.

HARDY: He'll be a better person for it.

CASH: She's ruined his life. She's taken away the beauty and the innocence of his childhood.

ROXY: Beauty and innocence?

CASH: We've reached the end of our relationship, Dad. You have set upon this boy to ruin him. I don't know why. Some idea, some twisted idea of yours to liberate him from all responsibility and common sense. It's my duty, to him, to take him away from you. I asked your girlfriend to help and this is how she helps.

HARDY: When did you ask her?

CASH: The other day, I had her over here for a visit, while you were out. I told her things about you, things she didn't know. And she told me things. And we agreed; it was better for Lowell to separate himself from you.

HARDY: Why would you agree to that? He's my grandson.

ROXY: You don't own him.

HARDY: I didn't say I owned him. Whose side are you on?

ROXY: You're going to die anyways! You're going to leave him. He loves you and you're going to just go and die on him!

He sees her struggling with it for the first time.

HARDY: Why are people so afraid of sadness?

ROXY: I couldn't tell you.

HARDY: We ought to welcome sadness. We ought to welcome death.

ROXY: Yeah, right.

HARDY: I thought you were tougher than that.

ROXY: Sure.

HARDY: I'm an old man anyway. This is what happens.

ROXY: Don't make it any easier.

HARDY: Are you crying?

ROXY: Just my hayfever.

HARDY: That's my girl.

ROXY: Anyways, I wouldn't separate the two of youse. You're best friends.

HARDY: Cash wants to press charges.

ROXY: For what?

LOWELL: It was a perfectly natural thing, Mom.

CASH: You're right; nothing more perfectly natural than a bipolar teenager and a radio hostess having casual sex in her apartment.

ROXY: Would somebody please tell that woman that it's a townhouse, not an apartment?

MILTON: She can tell it to the police.

ROXY: What's the point of locking me up when I live in this town?

MILTON: Maybe they'll make her a bargain.

LOWELL: She doesn't bargain.

MILTON: There's always a bargain.

LOWELL: I don't like it here. I want out of here.

MILTON: She cooperates—

LOWELL: She won't.

MILTON: Things get easier.

ROXY: Don't believe what people tell you.

LOWELL: Not even my own grandfather?

ROXY: Maybe you think too highly of him, Lowell. Maybe you shouldn't think so highly of him.

LOWELL: Why not?

ROXY: Nobody is perfect, least of all Hardy.

LOWELL: I know he's not perfect.

ROXY: Do you know he has cancer?

LOWELL is stung by the news.

HARDY: Why did you tell him?

ROXY: He thinks you're perfect; now he knows you're not.

HARDY: Did you tell him the rest?

49

ROXY: What "rest"; there is no "rest."

CASH: When did you find out?

HARDY: What difference does it make?

CASH: It would have been nice to know, that's all. Not nice. It would have been useful. It would have been—I could have prepared.

HARDY: You mean—made lunch?

CASH: I could have prepared myself emotionally.

HARDY: Why would you want to do that?

CASH: So I wouldn't—

She cries. He holds her for a moment.

HARDY: Cash?

CASH: What?

HARDY: I'm dying—not you.

CASH: Okay.

HARDY: While we're on the subject. I'd like you to do a little something for me.

CASH: Of course.

HARDY: You haven't heard what it is.

CASH: What is it?

HARDY: I want you to—make things easier for me.

ROXY: I told you not to say it.

HARDY: At the end.

ROXY: You shouldn't have said it.

CASH: What are you talking about?

HARDY: When the time comes. I don't want to linger and I don't want to suffer.

CASH: Dad—

HARDY: Like your mother, your poor mother.

CASH: I can't—allow that to happen.

HARDY: Do you want me to suffer?

CASH: No. I don't want you to suffer.

HARDY: Good.

CASH: But I can't—allow that. And neither can you. Your body, your life, it belongs to God.

ROXY: She's a certain kind of person.

LOWELL: If the peaches are too ripe, you can't eat them. They get bruised and soft.

MILTON: Why don't you try sticking with the subject, Lowell?

LOWELL: It is the subject. It's the subject.

HARDY: Peaches can't be left to rot, Lowell. There's a perfect time for picking, and after that time—

LOWELL: I love you, Grandpa.

HARDY: Don't say it.

LOWELL: But I do.

HARDY: I know you do. I know. But you can't love
something forever.

LOWELL: Why not?

HARDY: Because it goes away, and it's gone.

LOWELL: There's more to it than that, Mom says.

HARDY: There's no more to it.

LOWELL: Life is a gift, Mom says.

HARDY: Is that so? Who from?

CASH: It's a gift from God.

LOWELL: So how come we die?

CASH: I don't know.

LOWELL: If life is a gift from God, how come he takes it
back?

CASH: Death is also a gift.

LOWELL: It is?

CASH: If you believe in Heaven.

HARDY: Just smell that. Perfume. In the air.

They breathe it all in.

HARDY: Yup. It's time for me to go; I'm starting to regret things.

LOWELL: We shouldn't be here.

HARDY: Don't pay attention to rules all your life.

LOWELL: I try not to.

HARDY: Nobody owns this, Lowell.

LOWELL: We only own one thing in life, right?

HARDY: We own ourselves.

LOWELL: Property is capitalism.

CASH: Do you even know what that means?

LOWELL: Grandpa says I'll come to know.

CASH: Grandpa lost that land in a card game.

LOWELL: Is that true?

HARDY: No. Not all at once.

CASH: Slowly but surely gambled it all away.

LOWELL: This orchard was ours?

HARDY: Nothing is anybody's.

LOWELL: I thought you were a good card player.

HARDY: I was. My only weakness was that I stayed too long.

LOWELL: You need to know when to walk away.

HARDY: You need to know when to walk away, no matter how much you're up.

LOWELL: That's the hardest part of the game.

HARDY: The hardest part. Help me up here. I'm going to have one last look around.

LOWELL: Careful.

HARDY: I never really owned this. Nobody owns this. It belongs—to the ethos. Know what that is?

CASH: It's the same as God.

ROXY: Except he won't say God.

HARDY: This orchard is still ours, because we are still here; and when we're no longer here, it'll belong to those who follow us. Smell the air. That's our air. It's our time, Lowell. All ours.

LOWELL: Watch the ladder, Grandpa.

HARDY: A hundred years ago, we didn't matter; and hundred years from now, we won't matter again.

LOWELL: The ladder! Watch the ladder!

HARDY stumbles. Blackout.

2.

The play resumes. CASH addresses museum visitors.

CASH: The mill was opened in 1910. It was the first mill of its kind in the area. In 1925 it was purchased by A.R. Anderson, who relocated the mill from its original location upstream—

LOWELL: Mom?

CASH: —to where it now stands, albeit—

LOWELL: Mom!

CASH: —albeit abandoned. It was, it was renamed The Anderson Lumber Company after its new owner—

LOWELL: Mom!

CASH: What are you doing here?

LOWELL: There's been an accident.

CASH: Can't it wait?

LOWELL: An accident?

MILTON: Let's talk about it; let's talk about the accident.

LOWELL: Okay.

MILTON: He knew the ladder was broken, right?

LOWELL: You want me to tell you the truth?

MILTON: Yes.

LOWELL: The truth is relative; that's what my grandfather says.

HARDY: Is it a good card—ask yourself. An ace, for instance, can turn around and bite you in the ass.

ROXY: I don't know how.

LOWELL: What about three aces?

Beat.

HARDY: A good card blinds you to other possibilities. You get greedy, you think of your hand instead of your opponent's. As I say, it doesn't matter what's in your hand—not one little bit. Or your opponent's hand, either. I like a weak hand; it makes me forget about my own potential and makes me focus on the other guy. A good hand—like the one I happen to have at the moment— just lulls me into a false sense of certain victory. Look how lulled I am.

ROXY: You always look like that.

HARDY: Do I?

LOWELL: Yes.

ROXY: Besides, he's way up on you. He hardly needs any pointers.

HARDY: Natural talent needs to be nurtured, refined. You don't have three aces.

LOWELL: Don't I?

HARDY: Not if I've got two aces.

ROXY: Nobody believes you.

HARDY: Stay out of this.

LOWELL: Well, if you've got two aces, then you're right—I don't have three. So you haven't got anything to worry about.

HARDY: That's right.

LOWELL: Your bet.

HARDY: Fold.

LOWELL: King high.

MILTON: You said he knew it was broken.

LOWELL: I didn't say that.

HARDY: King high?

MILTON: Maybe you'd like to tell me what you said, then.

LOWELL: You're the one writing things down.

HARDY: You little bastard.

MILTON: That's correct. I'm writing things down, Lowell. I'm writing things down so that I have an exact record of what you said.

LOWELL: So then you don't need me to repeat it.

MILTON: I do need you to repeat it. I need you to say it again, the same way every time, so that I know it's consistent. Alright, let me help you out here a little. You said he knew the ladder was broken.

LOWELL: I don't remember.

MILTON: But you said it before. If it's true, how can you not remember?

LOWELL: I don't.

MILTON: "He knew it was broken, but he climbed it anyway." That's what you said.

LOWELL: Did you know that Alexander the Great died in his own vomit?

MILTON: I didn't know that.

HARDY: Always keep them guessing.

LOWELL: Even great men have humble endings.

MILTON: You know what murder is, right?

LOWELL: It's the Fifth Commandment.

MILTON: Did you murder your grandfather?

LOWELL: What do you think?

MILTON: I don't know what I think. I'm trying to get a picture.

LOWELL: I can't answer the question. I don't know what the truth is. What's the truth?

HARDY: I have about two or three months to live.

LOWELL: Two or three months?

HARDY: Just enough time to make me wish I wasn't alive.

LOWELL: I don't believe you; you're bluffing.

HARDY: Why, in God's name, would I bluff?

LOWELL: You tell me.

MILTON: Why would he bluff?

LOWELL: You tell me.

MILTON: If you thought he was bluffing, then why would you do it?

LOWELL: People do all kinds of things for all kinds of reasons.

MILTON: That's right, Lowell. That's why we interview people. That's why we ask the questions.

LOWELL: I don't have to answer your questions. I have the right to remain silent.

MILTON: Nobody's asking you to say anything.

LOWELL: So quit asking questions.

MILTON: I also have a right, Lowell. I have a right to ask questions, which you do not have to answer.

LOWELL: Can I go home now?

MILTON: Why would you kill him? Because you loved him? That doesn't make any sense to me.

LOWELL: I want to go home now.

MILTON: You might not be going home for a very long time, Lowell.

LOWELL: Let's make it not happen. Let's make it that it never happened.

MILTON: You loved your grandfather. Is that right?

LOWELL: No.

CASH: Yes you do.

MILTON: I don't believe you.

LOWELL: No!

Again, we see a different side of LOWELL, violent, out of control.

CASH: You're just upset. We're all upset, Lowell.

LOWELL: You're not. You want him dead.

CASH: What a thing to say.

LOWELL: You want him out of my life.

CASH: I want him out of your life, but I don't want him dead.

MILTON: Besides, she was at work at the time.

LOWELL: That's right.

MILTON: And anyway, she stood to gain nothing.

LOWELL shrugs.

HARDY: When I die, you get the house.

MILTON: What are you saying?

LOWELL: I'm not saying anything.

MILTON: You're saying your mother did it?

LOWELL: I'm not saying anything.

MILTON: A man is dead, Lowell. An investigation is underway to try and determine who fired the gun and why; and if a crime has been committed he or she will be found guilty and sentenced to a very long prison term. So imagine my surprise, with the stakes so high, Lowell, that you play games with me.

Beat.

Maybe you'd like me to repeat my original question.

LOWELL: I'm not playing games with you.

MILTON: Then let me repeat the question.

LOWELL: It wasn't a question.

MILTON: Alright, let me put it in the form of a question.

LOWELL: I don't have to answer your questions.

MILTON: Alright, it's not a question. I'm only wondering. Why would a woman kill her father to inherit a house she's going to inherit anyway? Does that make sense?

LOWELL: It doesn't have to make sense.

MILTON: How many different paths are we going to go down here, I wonder.

LOWELL: Is that a question?

HARDY: I'm only asking that you help me make it possible. And only when the time comes. When the pain is too much.

CASH: I can't believe you would even ask me that.

HARDY: Alright, I'm not asking you. I'm commanding you. Honour your father or something like that; isn't that a religious—?

CASH: They'll make you comfortable. You'll have time to— finish things.

HARDY: Finish things? What things? I'm finished.

LOWELL: Everybody has a death waiting for them.

MILTON: Let's go back to the orchard. Let's talk about the day he broke his leg.

LOWELL: I don't want to go back there. I don't ever want to.

MILTON: Let's go back. To the orchard.

LOWELL: Watch the ladder!

HARDY hits the ground. LOWELL runs to him.

HARDY: Damn it.

LOWELL: Can you move at all?

HARDY: No.

LOWELL: At least you didn't die from the fall, Grandpa.

HARDY: Why didn't I?

LOWELL: What?

HARDY: Never mind.

LOWELL: We need to get you to a hospital.

HARDY: Just leave me here. Go and get me the gun.

LOWELL: What?

HARDY: I don't want to go into any hospital. Do you understand?

LOWELL: I understand. But if your leg is broken, they have to fix it.

HARDY: That's right, Lowell; that's what they do. They fix it. They fix up everything. They keep it all going, even when there's no point. Because they're afraid, afraid of things dying. They're afraid of what happens.

LOWELL: Grandpa—

HARDY: You want to see me like this? A slow annihilation?

LOWELL: I don't know what to do.

CASH: So why did you just leave him there?

LOWELL: He wanted me to.

CASH: He could have died.

LOWELL: I never saw him look so old. Just lying there.
     Under the tree.

HARDY: This is where I want to die.

LOWELL: Okay.

HARDY: Don't tell your mother.

LOWELL: Okay.

MILTON: So why did you?

LOWELL: I don't know.

MILTON: You promised your grandfather; you went back on
     your word.

LOWELL: I didn't.

MILTON: I'm just trying to get some consistency here.

LOWELL: Okay.

CASH: Well, you did the right thing.

LOWELL: What happens now?

MILTON: That's up to you.

CASH: They make him better.

LOWELL: But he doesn't want to get better.

CASH: That's absurd.

LOWELL: It's a slow annihilation, Mom.

CASH: It's what life is.

LOWELL: You only say that because of Dad!

CASH: What?

LOWELL: You're unhappy and you think everybody else should be unhappy, too.

CASH, hurt, walks away.

Transition into hospital; HARDY is now in a wheelchair.

LOWELL: I brought you a deck of cards.

HARDY: No thanks.

LOWELL: I thought you might like to play.

HARDY: I've lost my fighting edge.

LOWELL: Are you mad at me?

HARDY: That nurse.

LOWELL: Which one?

HARDY: I think she likes me.

LOWELL: Her?

HARDY: I'm kidding. Nobody likes anybody in here.

LOWELL: You look tired.

HARDY: I am tired.

LOWELL: Cheer up, Grandpa.

HARDY: Did you bring me my magazines?

He hands HARDY some magazines from his collection.

LOWELL: I forgot to say one thing about the orchard. A few
days after the accident, I found a guy in there sleeping
under a tree. He said he was an angel. He said he came
from Heaven when I asked him.

HARDY: If Heaven is the nuthouse.

LOWELL: Maybe he came from the nuthouse and maybe
not. He appeared there for three days in a row, and then
he never appeared again. Grandpa didn't like it, but said
he was free to come and go as he pleased anyway, since
it was the nature of men to wander. I think that Grandpa
was afraid that if he was really an angel it would throw
his whole belief system into disorder.

HARDY: Go ask him: If there's a God, why does he treat men
so bad?

LOWELL: So I asked the man under the tree and he told me
the reason God treats men so bad is because they deserve
it. I don't think that's true. Do you think that's true?

MILTON: I don't—know.

CASH: You were in that orchard again?

LOWELL: I think that the reason God treats men so bad is
because he's just plain old mean.

CASH: Lowell, God loves us.

LOWELL: How do you know? Maybe he hates us.

CASH: Don't you know, sweetheart, that he loved the world so much he sacrificed his only begotten son?

LOWELL: Why didn't he sacrifice himself?

CASH: You think it's easy to sacrifice your only son?

LOWELL: For Dad it was.

CASH: What?

LOWELL: I said for Dad it was.

CASH: Your father—sends money every month. And anyway what's this got to do with God?

LOWELL: Ever since he left, you became a Christian.

CASH: I've been a Christian all my life. Once a week, I go to church.

LOWELL: Once a week, between ten-thirty and twelve-thirty, I have the house to myself, thanks to Christianity. Sometimes, I take the opportunity during those brief hours to sneak into Mom's room, which is strictly off limits, and try on some of Dad's clothes that he left. And then some of Mom's clothes. Sometimes, I pretend they're making love on the bed, and that's how I'm born. I have conversations about what kind of a name they'll choose for me. They always settle on Lowell, because my mother's grandfather came from there, in Massachusetts. Then they kiss and get all snuggly because they're so much in love. If only I didn't come along, they would probably still be married, but I created an economic imperative.

HARDY: Families cost money.

LOWELL: When the mill closed, my father suffered a personal crisis of inadequacy and therefore was incapable of emotional commitment.

CASH sighs.

LOWELL: So he ran off with Miss Hedley, who worked at the hardware store. She had dark hair. It had to be dark because my mother is blonde. It's all quite psychological. Mom tried dyeing her hair, but it was an unmitigated disaster and she cried. But she doesn't cry anymore.

CASH: You had no right to go in my room.

LOWELL: I had every right.

CASH: That's off limits.

LOWELL: It says in your will that Aunt Julie is my legal guardian in case of your demise.

CASH: I have to put someone.

LOWELL: Why not Dad?

CASH: He didn't want it to work out that way.

LOWELL: Why does he hate me?

CASH: He doesn't hate you.

LOWELL: He thinks I'm mentally retarded or something.

CASH: Your father doesn't have a lot of patience—for things.

LOWELL: What about Grandpa?

CASH: What about him?

LOWELL: Can't he be my legal guardian?

CASH: This is all hypothetical.

LOWELL: Not to me.

HARDY: Are you surprised? She never trusted me with you. I have aspirations for you that she doesn't share.

CASH: Those are my private papers.

LOWELL: Maybe I have my own aspirations.

HARDY: What?

LOWELL: My own aspirations.

HARDY: Sure you do.

MILTON: So you moved in with her.

ROXY: He needs a place of contemplation. Even a kid has to get his shit together.

LOWELL: Just for a few days.

CASH: Whose house?

LOWELL: My friend. You know. Can't I have a friend?

MILTON: Were you sleeping with her?

LOWELL: On and off. That's a joke of Grandpa's.

MILTON: I don't get it.

LOWELL: Sex is a private act between two people.

MILTON: Not if one of them is fifteen.

ROXY: I thought you were fourteen.

HARDY: They always go straight to the sex thing. It's their lowest common denominator. What counts is companionship. Roxy would say that, too.

ROXY: What counts is companionship.

LOWELL: I told Mom that I was staying with Freddy, the diabetic Jehovah's Witness, until he recovered from his appendicitis.

CASH: I thought it was a back injury.

LOWELL: The back injury is related to the appendicitis.

HARDY: Plausibility. Never give your opponent a chance to doubt you. Make it fast and make it feasible.

CASH: You'd better be telling me the truth.

HARDY: It's called the cushion of doubt. Allow your opponent to think what they want, but never change your story.

MILTON: But you are changing it.

ROXY: The truth, yeah. That's a rock nobody wants to look under. Big men with little brains and little women with big mouths. That's the truth. Small towns and small minds.

LOWELL: I know it.

ROXY: Do you?

LOWELL: Maybe I'm just going to get out of here. Go someplace.

ROXY: Doesn't change much, no matter where you go. Unless you plan on never getting involved with people.

LOWELL: I try not to.

ROXY: You are one sweet kid, Lowell. It hurts me just to think what the world's gonna do to you.

LOWELL: I can look after myself.

ROXY: Yeah? You gonna punch your way through life? You think life isn't gonna punch you right back? Here's a blanket. You're over there on the sofa.

MILTON: So you didn't sleep with her.

LOWELL: That would have been an abdication of my responsibilities. I was looking after her while Grandpa was in the hospital is all. She cooked eggs, naked, except for her slippers and a hat. She took baths in some kind of lemon juice. She watched *The Price Is Right* and ate Honey Bunches of Oats. She let me massage her feet with pink cream. We hung out for almost a week like that. And then one day—

ROXY: It's time we did something about your grandfather. He's been in there long enough. He can't die in a hospital.

(*as she exits*) Get my track pants.

LOWELL: The plan was to spring him. The plan was to take him back to the orchard, where I should have left him in the first place.

ROXY: Hey? Hey?

HARDY: Who are you?

ROXY: Roxy.

HARDY: I knew that.

ROXY: No you didn't.

HARDY: I've missed you. Who are you?

ROXY: Roxy.

LOWELL: He doesn't know who you are.

HARDY: Who's that?

ROXY: Leave us for a bit.

HARDY: Who's that?

ROXY: Lowell. Your grandson.

HARDY: Since when?

ROXY: Listen. I'm getting you out of here. Tomorrow, I'm
    getting you out of here.

HARDY: How?

ROXY: We're going to have a picnic.

HARDY: Roxy.

ROXY: That's right.

HARDY: Roxy.

ROXY: That's right.

HARDY: What the fuck is happening?

ROXY: Your cancer is spreading. It's all over.

HARDY: Is that why my leg feels broken?

ROXY: It is broken. You fell out of a tree.

HARDY: And got cancer?

ROXY: You already had the cancer.

HARDY: Roxy.

ROXY: Uh, huh?

HARDY: My wife died in this hospital.

ROXY: I know.

HARDY: I remember everything.

ROXY: I thought you couldn't remember anything.

HARDY: I remember—everything. Get me out of here.

ROXY: Tomorrow. We're going for a picnic.

HARDY: That was Lowell.

ROXY: He's living over at my townhouse.

HARDY: Let me talk to him.

LOWELL: I was scared to talk to him. He seemed like he was
gone to another place. That's what they say when they
don't want to say dead.

HARDY: I am gone to another place.

LOWELL: You're still here.

HARDY: In name only.

LOWELL: I'm going to get a job.

HARDY: Where?

LOWELL: I don't know. The Petro-Can?

HARDY: You can't be a gas pump jockey.

LOWELL: It's a stepping stone. (*out*) People come through here. That's one thing this place has always had going for it. It may be nowhere, but at least it's on the road to somewhere else. That's something to think about.

HARDY: Your mind is too interesting for that kind of work, Lowell.

LOWELL: It's because I'm unstable.

HARDY: You got a few screws loose; who doesn't? People try to name things. You have to name your own self. You are a special person; that's all you need to know.

LOWELL: I have a chemical imbalance.

HARDY: Sure; so long as you believe that, then you are giving over control of yourself to an idea. It's not the only truth, you know. You know what I said about getting dealt a bad hand. There's no such thing. No such thing. My father was missing a toe.

LOWELL: Really?

HARDY: He was missing a toe. He stood taller than any man I know. He stood like a man with eleven toes. I used to count them up for him. Yup, I'd say, there's only nine down here. He'd say, "The other one I cut off because I wanted to give myself something to think about." He was probably making that up, but if you knew my father, it was plausible enough. People have all kinds of imbalances in their life, Lowell. And they do just fine. You're going to be okay.

MILTON: It's not really true though, is it?

LOWELL: True enough.

MILTON: But you're not okay. You're in a lot of trouble.

LOWELL: You call it trouble; I call it something else.

LOWELL hands HARDY a pair of glasses.

Here.

HARDY: What are these?

LOWELL: I didn't have sunglasses, so I used a magic marker on your reading glasses.

HARDY: What for?

LOWELL: I thought you could use a disguise.

HARDY: If I'm walking out of here, I'm walking out of here my own man.

ROXY: If only he could walk.

HARDY: I'm rolling out, then. I don't have to hide who I am.

ROXY: Be quiet and keep your head down.

They stop cold, waiting for someone to pass.

LOWELL: The coast is clear.

ROXY: Just act normal.

LOWELL: Wait. There's somebody coming.

HARDY: To Hell with it. They can't keep me here.

LOWELL: But they did. We tried almost every day to get him out. It was always something.

CASH: You seem anxious.

HARDY: I am anxious.

CASH: You signed a "do not resuscitate" order.

HARDY: That's right.

CASH: Why?

HARDY: Are you out of your mind?

CASH: There are other people to consider besides yourself, you know.

HARDY: There are?

CASH: There's me. There's Lowell.

HARDY: I thought you didn't want me to have anything to do with Lowell.

CASH: He's your grandson. He doesn't want to see you die at the very first opportunity. He needs closure.

HARDY: I don't.

CASH: We all need closure.

HARDY: What for?

CASH: There are things. Things that were never said.

HARDY: By who?

CASH: Well, me, for one. Don't you have anything you'd like to say?

HARDY: About what?

CASH: I don't know. You're dying. You must have something you want to say. Something you've always wanted to tell me.

HARDY: Alright, there is something I want to tell you. Since you're forcing me into it.

CASH: I'm not forcing you. What is it?

HARDY: I don't—Cash, I have to be honest. I can't die without letting you know this. I don't like your banana bread.

CASH: My what?

HARDY: I have to say, it doesn't taste even remotely like bananas. And it's heavy and soggy. I feel, when I've eaten it, I always feel like I've eaten—a wet paper towel. There. I've said it. Now let me die in peace.

CASH: I'm sure there's more you want to say than that.

HARDY: When you were a little girl, you used to come running up to me and throw yourself right at me. I mean leap right up a little into the air and suspend yourself in anticipation. You always knew I would catch you and swing you around. You never for a second doubted it. Then I thought one day, I thought,"I can't have you believing in this. I can't have you believing that a man, any man, will catch you at a moment's notice. Because that's the kind of belief that takes away a person's strength, gives it over to others." So that day I didn't catch you. Do you remember?

CASH: No.

HARDY: That day, the day I thought about it, I let you go. You fell down in front of me and cried and cried. Mom said, "Why the Hell didn't you catch her?" I stood there and saw that look on your face and, as hard as it was and as cruel, I knew I'd taught you something. I knew that I had taught you not to rely on other people so much. Especially men. And now I see you and I see how strong you've become and how independent, how self-reliant, and how much your own person, and I realize, Cash— that I was wrong. I should have caught you. Because I took away from you the one thing you need in your life. Belief in other people.

CASH: I believe in other people.

HARDY: I guess that's why you have a gun in the house.

CASH: Things happen, even in this town.

HARDY: The thief already came and went.

CASH: Don't be cryptic.

HARDY: I think his name was Connor.

CASH: Are you trying to hurt me?

HARDY: You don't believe in Lowell.

CASH: Lowell is different.

HARDY: Of course he is. You make that story up in your head so you can intrude on his life.

CASH: He's my son.

HARDY: And he's my grandson. And I find it very hard, sometimes, to imagine how he'll get along in this world, but I have to imagine that he will. I have to imagine, too, that the world will carry on, much the way it has, long after us, and that people will come and go, in ordinary fashion. And trees will grow and fruit will fall and life will happen over and over again. It's hard to think of yourself not in the world. You get this feeling, when you're younger, you get this feeling that you own the world, but you realize, as years go by, that time is the possessor of all things.

CASH: You mean God. You're talking about God again.

HARDY: I most certainly am not.

CASH: You call it time, and you call it the ethos, or whatever, but you're talking about God.

HARDY: Why is it so important to you?

CASH: Because in spite of your desire for me to be independent and think my own thoughts, you have never let me think them. My belief in God, for one.

HARDY: I don't stop you.

CASH: You make fun of me instead. But that's okay, Dad, because I see through you. I always suspected you were a Christian underneath all that atheism.

HARDY: If anything must be said before I die, Cash, it's this: I don't believe in God, but I'd be happy to make his acquaintance.

CASH: I don't remember you dropping me.

HARDY: I might have made that up.

CASH: I can't imagine you ever dropping me.

HARDY: Come to think of it, neither can I.

A beat of tenderness; MILTON breaks the mood.

MILTON: Father and daughter reconciled. What a beautiful story.

CASH: I love you, Dad.

HARDY: Why do you have to say it?

CASH: Because we're not very good at telling each other.

HARDY: It's enough to know.

CASH: But if we don't tell each other, we'll never know.

MILTON: I can understand why that would be the perfect moment, a nice ending to it all.

LOWELL: You have to stop talking now.

MILTON: Messy. Life is so messy, isn't it?

LOWELL: I'll tell you the truth now.

MILTON: If only we could control it. If only we could call the time and place.

LOWELL: I'll tell you the whole truth.

MILTON: People could get their lives in order. They could, well, they could really organize.

LOWELL: I'll tell you the truth.

MILTON: I'm not so sure you can.

CASH: Oh. And I heard about this lawyer.

HARDY: What'd you hear?

CASH: I heard you talked to one.

HARDY: I might have.

CASH: Why on earth are you talking to a lawyer?

HARDY: You leave a ladder around in an orchard, Cash, you've got to assume a certain legal responsibility.

CASH: You were on somebody else's property. Anyway, you're too sick to fight a legal case at this point.

HARDY: It can be fought long after me.

CASH: What do you gain by it then?

HARDY: Not me. You. And the boy.

CASH: You can't win this case.

HARDY: We have a good shot at an out-of-court deal.

CASH: We?

HARDY: Everything goes to you.

CASH: I can take care of myself.

MILTON: And that was her last word on the subject?

CASH: That is absolutely my last word on the subject, Dad.

HARDY: Okay. But think about Lowell.

CASH: This isn't about Lowell.

HARDY: The Andersons ruined us, Cash. They took responsibility for nothing and no one; they drained this town for all it was worth, and left. They destroyed our lives.

CASH: They destroyed your life. Everybody else has moved on.

She leaves. He calls after her.

HARDY: Where exactly have you moved on to?

LOWELL: That was the last thing he ever said to her.

MILTON: Are you sure of that?

LOWELL: Pretty positive. We came in right after and we took him away.

MILTON: To the orchard.

ROXY: Picnic time!

LOWELL: It was the twenty-first of September. We took my grandfather for his last visit to the Anderson orchard. He was very sick at the time, but he wanted to get out of the hospital. He wanted to eat peaches. We drove in a car. It was a car that Roxy had borrowed from a radio listener.

ROXY: I got a few fans out there.

LOWELL: It was a warm day. We folded the wheelchair into the trunk of the car. A nurse passed us on her way into the hospital, but she just nodded and smiled and we nodded and smiled back. We peeled out of there, drove about a million miles an hour out of town. Dirt and rocks just flying out from under the car. Roxy came to a screeching halt at the Anderson house. Everything was quiet. We got out of the car and wheeled Grandpa around back of the house to where the orchard began.

HARDY: Smell that.

ROXY: I can't smell anything.

LOWELL: I couldn't either.

HARDY: That is the smell of Heaven.

LOWELL: I thought you didn't believe in Heaven.

HARDY: Heaven is right here on earth, Lowell. On earth.

ROXY: Just keep reminding yourself of that.

LOWELL: Then the first of his pain started.

HARDY: Freestone are the best for eating fresh. Here. Try one.

ROXY: Did I ever tell you, honey, that I don't like peaches?

Struggling with his pain.

HARDY: This is what it's going to be like.

ROXY: That's right.

HARDY: How long, I wonder.

LOWELL: Mom says they'll give you morphine.

HARDY: I'll die a gibbering idiot; I'll say things I don't mean to say.

ROXY: I don't like peaches. I always think I'm eating soap.

HARDY: I'm not sure I care much for the flavour of them, either. But I like the provenance.

ROXY: Free, is what he means, I think.

HARDY: Free is exactly what I mean.

LOWELL: We sat and ate peaches, even though we all finally agreed that we didn't much care for the taste of them. It was the experience.

ROXY: I find them sensual, if nothing else.

LOWELL: And Grandpa's pain went away, for a bit.

HARDY: Imagine owning all this and never bothering with it. Never coming around to visit. Ever.

ROXY: We should be grateful.

HARDY: You're right, as always, baby. If they were here, I suppose we wouldn't be. It's only by virtue of their neglect that we lay any claim to this property at all.

ROXY: Lay claim, do you?

HARDY: To this, and all of this.

LOWELL: I thought you didn't believe in ownership.

HARDY: I claim it on behalf of all humankind, or at least those that live in this thankless valley. From this day forward, the Anderson orchard shall be named the People's Orchard. And no one but the people shall be allowed on it. All others are trespassers. You hear that, Lowell?

LOWELL: I hear. (*out*) I also heard, at that very moment, the sound of a car approaching.

MILTON: Your mother.

LOWELL: My mother was at work.

HARDY: Go check and see who it is, Lowell. Roxy and I have some things to talk over here.

LOWELL: I walked out of the orchard and toward the house. I could see somebody getting out of a blue pick-up truck—

MILTON: You said "a car."

HARDY: Stick with your story.

LOWELL: I couldn't see who he was exactly; he had a slight limp. He was wearing blue jeans and he had a rifle with him. I ducked down behind some crates so he couldn't see me. I could hear him try the front door of the house. I guess he was going to rob it. I stayed very quiet. He went around the back, near to where I was, but he still didn't see me. I was breathing so hard, I could practically have split in two.

MILTON: He tried the front door, you say.

LOWELL: And the back door. He walked around the house a couple of times and then he broke a window. I ran back to tell Grandpa.

HARDY: Who is he?

LOWELL: A robber, I think.

ROXY: Leave it be.

HARDY: Take me up there and I'll have a word with this fellow. He goes busting up the Anderson house, before you know it, they'll be back here, safeguarding it against us. There's no greater cause for the rich than the exertion of their property rights.

ROXY: I think we should all just stay here.

HARDY: He has a gun, you say?

LOWELL: I think it was.

HARDY: Could be a dangerous fellow.

ROXY: Stay here.

LOWELL: Grandpa wouldn't listen to her.

MILTON: What colour was this truck again?

LOWELL: I believe I said it was blue.

MILTON: He had a limp.

LOWELL: Left leg.

MILTON: How would you know that?

LOWELL: Huh?

MILTON: How would you know left or right? When a person has a limp, it's pretty hard to tell.

LOWELL: Educated guess.

MILTON: A blue truck.

LOWELL: That's right.

MILTON: I guess most trucks, blue or otherwise, leave tracks.

LOWELL: Not if they park in the tall grass.

MILTON: You didn't say he parked in the tall grass.

LOWELL: It didn't seem important.

MILTON: If you're suggesting that somebody—we don't know who—came out of nowhere, with a rifle, and for no reason whatsoever limped toward your grandfather, on his right leg—

LOWELL: I believe I said left—

MILTON: —and for no reason shot your grandfather, in cold blood, then I think every little detail is important, Lowell.

LOWELL: I didn't say no reason. There was a reason.

MILTON: What was that?

LOWELL: My grandfather was on private property.

MILTON: What are you saying?

LOWELL: I'm only correcting you, sir. You said there was no reason. I'm providing you with one.

MILTON: You're saying this was Mr. Anderson.

LOWELL: I don't know Mr. Anderson.

MILTON: I don't think Mr. Anderson would appreciate any suggestion that he shot somebody on his own land. Just for being there.

LOWELL: Do you know him?

MILTON: Let's talk about something else. Let's talk about your condition.

LOWELL: I don't have a condition.

CASH: It's completely treatable.

MILTON: I believe you take drugs for it. Lithium, I believe.

HARDY: Hold your cards like this. Up—like this. Remember, the cards are irrelevant. It's what's in your head.

LOWELL: I don't have a condition.

MILTON: It's easy enough for me to check with your doctor. In fact, I already have.

LOWELL: I doubt it.

MILTON: Oh?

LOWELL: If you'd checked with my doctor he wouldn't have told you I have any kind of condition because my doctor is not equipped to make that kind of diagnosis.

HARDY: Plausibility.

MILTON: I'm sure it's very hard sometimes to deal with depression. You haven't got a lot of outlets. I hear you tried to kill yourself.

LOWELL: You heard wrong.

MILTON: So everything your mother told me about you is untrue.

LOWELL: I don't know what my mother told you. But she's prone to exaggeration.

MILTON: Why would you kill your grandfather if you loved him?

LOWELL: That's a good question.

HARDY: Stay here, Roxy. There's no need for you to go.

ROXY: Are you crazy? He's got a gun.

HARDY: But he doesn't know that I haven't got one.

ROXY: You're going to bluff the guy?

HARDY: Let's go.

LOWELL: As I wheeled him up to the house, he reached around and grabbed hold of my hand. He held onto it tight. We stopped for a second. It was the last time he ever spoke to me.

HARDY: Don't stay in this town. Don't let this town take hold of you. Go someplace. Go anyplace.

LOWELL: Where?

HARDY: You'll figure out where. You'll find yourself places; you'll make yourself a reason for being there. When there's no more reason, you'll move on. You can't let one place own you. You have to go places you don't belong. You have to do things you have no right to do. You have to step over boundaries and walk past signs and keep going. That's the way to live; the rest is servitude.

LOWELL: I have a condition, Grandpa.

HARDY: You have no condition. Your condition is life. That's your condition.

LOWELL: Okay.

HARDY: And when you're cured of that condition, it's over. That's it. Fold.

LOWELL: Okay.

HARDY: Where is this guy?

LOWELL: Maybe inside.

HARDY: You go around the front.

MILTON: You're a young man.

LOWELL: That's right.

MILTON: You've got your whole life ahead of you.

LOWELL: That's right.

MILTON: How do you suppose you'll do in there?

LOWELL: I'll do okay.

MILTON: You won't crack under the pressure?

LOWELL: I don't think so.

MILTON: You need to take an oath.

LOWELL: I know.

MILTON: You need to swear to tell the truth.

LOWELL: The truth is relative.

MILTON: Not in court it isn't.

LOWELL: The truth is relative.

MILTON: You could bargain.

LOWELL: See, I told you.

MILTON: You could make a plea, now, ahead of time, and
    things would go better for you.

LOWELL: I know.

MILTON: Otherwise, it'll all come out at the inquest.

LOWELL: There are trees in rows.

MILTON: The gun registered to your mother—

LOWELL: Trees all in exact rows.

CASH: That gun disappeared. Some time ago.

LOWELL: They're lined up, one after the other.

MILTON: You being right there at the scene—

LOWELL: Fruit-bearing trees, heavy with their peaches.

MILTON: You'll be charged.

LOWELL: And the fruit falls to the ground and we pick it up—

HARDY: Here's a picture of me when I was your age.

LOWELL: I look just like you.

HARDY: Just like me.

LOWELL: That's the Anderson orchard.

HARDY: Before it was the Anderson orchard. That's me, standing under a tree.

LOWELL: The peaches look exactly the same.

HARDY: They always will.

LOWELL: Who's this?

HARDY: That's my father.

LOWELL: Are you stealing peaches?

HARDY: Nope. Just standing there.

LOWELL: That was a long time ago.

HARDY: I can still remember it.

LOWELL: Yeah, I can remember it, too.

HARDY: You weren't even there.

LOWELL: I know.

HARDY: You're a little soft in the head, Lowell.

LOWELL: Keep them guessing.

HARDY: That's my boy.

LOWELL recites, in somewhat rehearsed fashion—

LOWELL: On the afternoon of the twenty-first of September, I left my grandfather at the back of the Anderson house and I went around to the front. The sun was shining. It was warm. I peeked in through the front window to see what I could see inside. Suddenly, I heard a shot ring out. For a second I was stunned and I didn't move, and then I saw a blue truck take off from the premises. It had been parked in the grass. I ran around to the back of the house and that's where I discovered my grandfather, lying on the ground, bleeding. He had a smile on his face. It looked kind of weird, I remember thinking. My mother always said we would get caught trespassing. I guess she was right.

ROXY: It was the only way to go.

CASH: There's no evidence to suggest anything conclusive.

ROXY: Just a whole lot of possibilities.

LOWELL: I saw a guy in a blue truck is all.

CASH: I was at work at the time.

ROXY: I heard a gunshot. I think I heard a vehicle.

LOWELL: And that's all I know.

CASH: Murder is against God's law.

ROXY: Cause of death—

LOWELL: It's the Fifth Commandment; is that right, Mom?

ROXY: Undetermined.

CASH: Our lives belong to God, and God will take them
when he sees fit.

ROXY: And anyway, why would you kill someone you
loved?

ROXY and CASH disappear.

MILTON: Good question.

MILTON disappears with his briefcase.

LOWELL: I looked at him, just lying there in all that blood.
He smiled at me, kind of. I said, "You wonder why it has
to end. You wonder, Grandpa." "No," he said—

HARDY: You don't wonder. It just does.

HARDY appears behind LOWELL.

You hold on, you do your best; at the end of the night,
you cash in your chips and you go home.

HARDY hands LOWELL some magazines and his cap.

LOWELL: This is your home.

HARDY: That's right, Lowell.

HARDY wanders away.

LOWELL: I read about a crime in one of Grandpa's stash of crime magazines—an old man murdered his wife because she was sick and he didn't want her to suffer.

HARDY: There's no crime in that.

HARDY begins to disappear into the trees. CASH appears with a duffel bag for LOWELL.

CASH: I'm sending you to a place where they can look after you, Lowell; and we'll hear no more about this.

She kisses him and goes.

LOWELL: I'm going away where they can look after me, and that'll be the end of it. Except for one more thing. I saw Grandpa stand up, I mean right there—I'm not kidding—I saw him stand up, out of that pool of blood he was lying in, and walk right back into the orchard. I'm not kidding about this. He walked back into the orchard. He took a peach off a tree and kept walking, until he was gone.

HARDY disappears. A single light on LOWELL. He smiles. Blackout.

The end.